SCENAS INFANTIS

For Piano

By
OCTAVIO PINTO

■

Ed. 1512

G. SCHIRMER, Inc.

DISTRIBUTED BY

7777 W. BLUEMOUND RD. P.O. BOX 13819 MILWAUKEE, WI 53213

To Anna Maria and Luiz Octavio

I.

Brincam as creanças no jardim
os seus folguedos infantis.
Na rua passa o ceguinho
cantando as suas tristezas.

II.

Vamos brincar de roda? . . .
«Muito bom dia
Vossa Senhoria
Mada - o - tiro - tiro - lá . . .»

III.

Olha os soldadinhos
em marcha para o quartel!
«Marcha soldado
Cabeça de papel. . .»

IV.

Cae a tarde.
O Cuco bate seis horas,
e as meninas cantam,
ninando as bonecas,
«Dorme Nenêm.
Que a cuca já ahi vem . . .»

V.

Termina a grande folia,
e saltando de alegria
recolhem-se, engarupadas,
nos cavallinhos de páu.

I.

The garden is full of life.
In the sunshine children run about
Gaily and noisily.
Outside, on the street,
The poor blind man with his hand-organ
Sings his sorrows.

II.

"Let's play ring-around-the-rosie,"
Says little Anna Maria.
Quickly they form a ring
Singing and dancing.

III.

At the other corner,
Little Luiz Octavio comes marching by,
With his men, in paper hats,
Carrying wooden guns.

IV.

The sun falls down the west,
Six times sings the Cuckoo in the clock.
The little girls sing lullabies,
Sing that their dollies must go to sleep
Before the bogey-man comes!

V.

And now play-time is over,
And the children
Come prancing happily home
On their wooden hobby-horses.

Run, run!

Octavio Pinto

36182

4

The Organ-Grinder passes by

fading away

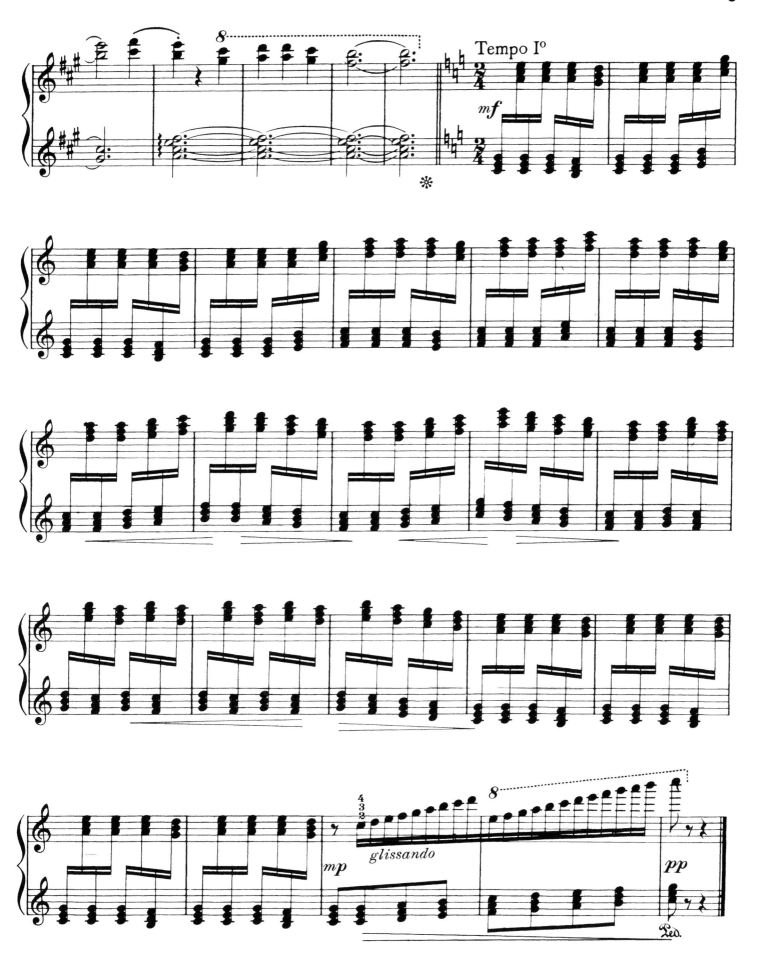

Ring around the rosy!
Roda-roda

March, little soldier!

Marcha, Soldadinho

Sleeping Time

Six times sings the cuckoo in the clock

Piano

Slowly and expressively

Lullaby

rall.

"Too-hoo," says the Owl

pp

l.h.

Quickly and shrilly

Ma - ma!

f

p rit. e dim. molto pp

Ped.

Tempo Iº

sleepily

ppp

rall. molto

rall.

Hobby-horse
Salta, Salta